TRANSFORMATION
OF A MAN'S

TRANSFORMATION

Howard Baker, Gordon Dalbey
and Stephen W. Smith

SIX SESSIONS FOR INDIVIDUALS OR GROUPS

IVP Connect

An imprint of InterVarsity Press
Downers Grove, Illinois

InterVarsity Press
P.O. Box 1400, Downers Grove, IL 60515-1426
World Wide Web: www.ivpress.com
E-mail: mail@ivpress.com

InterVarsity Press® is the book-publishing division of InterVarsity Christian Fellowship/USA®, a student movement active on campus at hundreds of universities, colleges and schools of nursing in the United States of America, and a member movement of the International Fellowship of Evangelical Students. For information about local and regional activities, write Public Relations Dept., InterVarsity Christian Fellowship/USA, 6400 Schroeder Rd., P.O. Box 7895, Madison, WI 53707-7895, or visit the IVCF website at <www.intervarsity.org>.

Design: Cindy Kiple
Images: Alan Kearney / Getty Images

ISBN-10: 0-8308-2148-1
ISBN-13: 978-0-8308-2148-8

Printed in the United States of America ∞

P	19	18	17	16	15	14	13	12	11	10	9	8	7	6	5	4	3	2	1
Y	21	20	19	18	17	16	15	14	13	12	11	10	09	08	07	06			

CONTENTS

INTRODUCTION

Too often we are like strangers in our own house. Asked why we think, feel and act in a certain way, we find we have no answer.

Sometimes our only answer is to try to change—to think, feel or act differently. But changes that we force ourselves to make are short-lived, and we find ourselves repeating our history with still no ready explanation. At best we muster up the strength to make changes to our circumstances, but we remain frustrated in our hearts.

The journey toward transformation is all about reshaping our hearts; not the muscle in our chest but what Henri Nouwen calls "our hidden center"—often hidden even from us. We keep our distance from it, as though what holds the passion inside of us is what frightens us most.

That is the painful part of being human. We fail to know our hidden center and our submerged parts, so we live and die without knowing who we really are. We are strangers in our own house.

The four Transformation of a Man's Heart discussion guides help us to get our house in order. More than just a Bible study, these guides help us to explore the distinctives of the masculine heart and move us toward authentic transformation into the men God wants us to become.

Each session begins with an excerpt from the book *The Transformation of a Man's Heart,* compiled and edited by Stephen W. Smith.

This passage can be read individually or aloud in a group setting. It isn't necessary to read the book before going through this guide, but you may want to read the book for a more in-depth exploration of how God transforms a man's life.

Sessions are divided into five different sections, each of which helps you focus on a different aspect of your heart. "Examining My Story" offers reflective questions and exercises that help prepare us for the topic, theme and heartfelt need that will be addressed. "Engaging the Scriptures" is a guided study of a particular section of Scripture with questions and comments. "Experiencing the Journey" is a practical application of what has just been studied.

This convergence of thought, Scripture and reflection will help equip us for what lies ahead. "Expressing Our Hearts to God" offers creative ways of praying about the subject. And occasional "Encouragements from Other Companions" run alongside each session to reassure us that our experience is authentic and transformation is possible.

SUGGESTIONS FOR INDIVIDUAL USE

If you have chosen to use this guide individually, you can move at your own pace from session to session, taking as much time as you like working through the questions, journaling your responses and taking notes. Consider using a simple spiral-bound journal to elaborate on your answers. Allow yourself to reflect on the issues that are raised. Each session is designed to be a guided journey into the truth of God's Word and the issues of a man's heart.

1. As you begin each session, pray that God will speak to you through his Word.

2. Read the introduction to the session and respond to the personal reflection questions under "Examining My Story." These are designed to help you focus on God and on the theme of the session.

3. "Engaging the Scriptures" deals with a particular biblical passage. Read and reread the passage to be studied. Unless otherwise indicated, the questions are written using the language of the New International Version, so you may wish to use that version of the Bible. *The Message* is also recommended.

4. It might be good to have a Bible dictionary handy. Use it to look up any unfamiliar words, names or places.

5. Take your time working through "Experiencing the Journey." The witness of the Bible and the work of the Spirit may converge in your heart during this time. Be honest with yourself and open to change.

6. Use the prayer suggestion to guide you in thanking God for what you have learned and to pray about the applications that have come to mind.

SUGGESTIONS FOR GROUP MEMBERS

Small groups and classes make excellent forums for rich discussion; this guide will help a group get to some of the core issues facing men today. Lively discussion should be welcomed, and every member of your group should strive to create a safe environment for each other to share openly and deeply about issues of the heart.

A safe environment for men is fostered by setting certain ground rules which should be agreed on prior to the group's beginning. Here are some suggested ground rules to think through prior to beginning your group:

1. Be willing to participate in the discussion. The leader will be asking the questions that are found in this guide. The leader can really become more of a guide than a teacher, helping navigate the discussion that will result from the study. The sessions will "teach" themselves. Group members will also help teach each other.

2. Stick to the topic being discussed. This allows for everyone to par-

ticipate in in-depth study on equal ground.

3. Be sensitive to the other members of the group. Listen attentively when they describe what they have learned. You may be surprised by their insights! Many questions do not have "right" answers, particularly questions that aim at meaning or application.

4. Jesus modeled acceptance throughout his interaction with people. Paul reminds us to "accept one another just as Christ accepted you" (Romans 15:7). Feeling accepted without the threat of feeling judged is key to helping men relax and share their story and heart struggles. In the group, be affirming whenever you can. This will encourage some of the more hesitant members of the group to participate.

5. Be careful not to dominate the discussion. We are sometimes so eager to express our thoughts that we leave too little opportunity for others to respond. By all means participate! But allow others to also. Everyone needs to be heard, and if we can make sure that all hearts are heard when we do the study, we'll meet a deeper goal of actually being a "group" or community.

6. Expect God to teach you through the passage being discussed and through the other members of the group. Pray that you will have an enjoyable and profitable time together, but also that as a result of each session you will find ways that you can participate in God's work transforming your life.

7. Confidentiality is important to create a safe environment. Decide together who the group members will tell. Will spouses or other friends know what is shared in the group? Anything said in the group should not be discussed outside the group unless specific permission is given to do so.

If you are the group leader, you will find additional suggestions and help at the back of the guide.

THE PROCESS OF TRANSFORMATION

Transformation is *never* complete. I am no trophy of transformation, only a man in the process of transformation. I can only confess (and you can confess with me):

God uses flawed men to accomplish his purposes.

I am a flawed man.

I am a man in process.

God is using me now and will continue to use me in the future to accomplish what he desires.

I am not perfect, but I am available.

Come, O God, and transform my heart.

The real transformation of a man involves his heart. If we are to be transformed, God must have access to that sacred place within. Let the transformation begin!

"AM I EVER GOING TO CHANGE?"

One evening, Dave's wife "caught" him staring into the computer screen in the middle of the night in the basement office. Dave had escaped there to enter the dark hole of cyber pornography. Once confronted by his wife through angry tears, Dave promised to ". . . never do *it* again." He meant it too. He was almost relieved. Yet, within days, Dave secretly slipped off to the basement after making sure his wife was asleep to revisit—just this once. He wrestled with guilt yet returned again and again. He simply couldn't stop.

The journey toward transformation is scattered with people who have tried and tried and yet failed time and time again. We also know people who *act* as if they have changed but continue to struggle in private, or when held accountable, are tempted to lie and cover up their failings. We can become suspicious or cynical, wondering if we can every really change at all.

Moving toward authentic transformation is one of the goals of the Christian life. We either change or we remain the same. And for some of us, that's a pretty scary thought.

EXAMINING MY STORY

1. How would you describe your efforts to change yourself over the past few years?

2. What does the struggle to change look like for you?

3. What area of your life would you like to see change in?

I need to be transformed because I know what it is like to not be transformed.

ANONYMOUS MAN IN A SMALL GROUP

ENGAGING THE SCRIPTURES
Romans 7:18-24

[18]I know that nothing good lives in me, that is, in my sinful nature. For I have the desire to do what is good, but I cannot carry it out. [19]For what I do is not the good I want to do; no, the evil I do not want to do—this I keep on doing. [20]Now if I do what I do not want to do, it is no longer I who do it, but it is sin living in me that does it.

[21]So I find this law at work: When I want to do good, evil is right there with me. [22]For in my inner being I delight in God's law; [23]but I see another law at work in the members of my body, waging war against the law of my mind and making me a prisoner of the law of sin at work within my members. [24]What a wretched man I am! Who will rescue me from this body of death?

4. Try paraphrasing Paul's words in the space provided here. Share what you feel is appropriate with the other group members.

5. How does looking into Paul's heart make you feel?

6. How does Paul's struggle compare to your own?

It is never too late to become what you might have been.

GEORGE ELIOT

7. It's easy to say, "Jesus changed my life." But Paul doesn't allow us to escape the reality of the struggle. How does this struggle play out? Is transformation instant or more gradual? Explain.

8. What does it mean to be rescued or delivered from the struggle by Jesus?

EXPERIENCING THE JOURNEY

9. What do repeated failures in trying to change do to us as men?

10. Describe someone you've seen successfully change. What was their struggle like?

Growth is the only evidence of life.

JOHN HENRY NEWMAN

11. How are you hoping Jesus will rescue or liberate you? What stands in the way?

EXPRESSING OUR HEARTS TO GOD

Use the following prayer as a guide as you talk to God about your efforts and desires to be transformed.

"Gracious and loving God, you know the deep inner patterns of my life that keep me from being totally yours. You know the misformed structures of my being that hold me in bondage to something less than your high purpose for my life. You also know my reluctance to let you have your way with me in these areas. Hear the deeper cry for wholeness, and by your grace enable me to be open to your transforming presence."

Try writing your own prayer expressing your need of transformation to God. You may find the words of a song, chorus or hymn helpful.

REAL CHANGE

Can we really cover things up? Can a well-made, tailored jacket cover 45 pounds? Can a quick smile cover the rage we just expressed? Can warning the family that "we don't talk about this outside this house" hide the lurking dysfunction?

A good mirror reveals the truth about every man. But we have to look into that mirror. The journey to transformation begins with the desire to look at and own the truth about myself. But how does a man really change? Does this happen in community, church or alone? Is there a specific formula to follow? These are the questions we find ourselves wrestling with as men.

The journey to transformation continues as I face the *larger* truth that I am unable to permanently change myself without the power of God. If I could have, I would have. Nothing short of this sincere desire for change will launch us on the path toward transformation.

EXAMINING MY STORY

1. Read the table below. Write down your own thoughts and feelings about your own journey toward transformation in the space provided.

Transformation Worksheet

Authentic Transformation *Important ingredients in the process and journey*	Pseudo-transformation *Where we've been before—previously explored territory*	Your Story
Faces the truth: I want to experience authentic transformation in a specific area (John 8:31-32; Romans 7:15-25)	Perpetuates a lie and excuses behavior: • "I don't have a problem." • "Everyone does this."	
Admits brokenness: I cannot change myself. I need God's help to truly transform. It is beyond my own strength or abilities. (2 Corinthians 4:7-12)	Portrays a polished façade: • "There's nothing wrong with me." • "Everyone else is doing this."	
Embraces a process: Transformation is not a quick fix. Becoming like Jesus involves time and mistakes. (Jeremiah 18:1-6; 2 Corinthians 3:18; Ephesians 4:13-15; 1 John 3:2)	Frantically looks for quick answers: • steps • logic • laws • tips • techniques	
Requires surrender and humility: I can't do it alone. God, please help me. (Matthew 26:39; James 4:10; 1 Peter 5:6)	Insists on self-help and self-reliance. Keeps the struggle a secret.	

Authentic Transformation *Important ingredients in the process and journey*	Pseudo-transformation *Where we've been before— previously explored territory*	Your Story
Inside-out change: Authentic transformation requires more than changing on the surface. (Matthew 23:25; Mark 7:18-23)	Outside, external change: • preoccupied with appearances • concerned with reputation. • "What will others think of me?"	
Collaborative and cooperative: I need encouragement, help and accountability to experience authentic transformation. I cannot do this by myself. (Ecclesiastes 4:9-12; Matthew 18:19-20; Philippians 2:12)	Competitive and judgmental: • desperado/Lone Ranger mentality • critical of others who seem far behind • ungracious toward others who fail	
Personalized process: What works for you may not work for me. Trusting that God knows me and is familiar with all my ways means that God knows what I need for change. (Psalm 139:13-15)	Cookie-cutter: • "If I could find the right program or method, I'd really change." • "I'll wait till the next book or program comes out."	

2. How do you see pseudo-transformation lived out in others? In yourself?

3. Why is admitting our inability to fix ourselves important? What does it take for a man to make such an admission?

If you would attain to what you are not yet, you must always be displeased by what you are. For where you are pleased with yourself there you have remained. Keep adding, keep walking, keep advancing.

SAINT AUGUSTINE

ENGAGING THE SCRIPTURES
Luke 15:11-32

[11]Jesus continued: "There was a man who had two sons. [12]The younger one said to his father, 'Father, give me my share of the estate.' So he divided his property between them.

[13]"Not long after that, the younger son got together all he had, set off for a distant country and there squandered his wealth in wild living. [14]After he had spent everything, there was a severe famine in that whole country, and he began to be in need. [15]So he went and hired himself out to a citizen of that country, who sent him to his fields to feed pigs. [16]He longed to fill his stomach with the pods that the pigs were eating, but no one gave him anything.

[17]"When he came to his senses, he said, 'How many of my father's hired men have food to spare, and here I am starving to death! [18]I will set out and

go back to my father and say to him: Father, I have sinned against heaven and against you. [19]I am no longer worthy to be called your son; make me like one of your hired men.' [20]So he got up and went to his father.

"But while he was still a long way off, his father saw him and was filled with compassion for him; he ran to his son, threw his arms around him and kissed him.

[21]"The son said to him, 'Father, I have sinned against heaven and against you. I am no longer worthy to be called your son.'

[22]"But the father said to his servants, 'Quick! Bring the best robe and put it on him. Put a ring on his finger and sandals on his feet. [23]Bring the fattened calf and kill it. Let's have a feast and celebrate. [24]For this son of mine was dead and is alive again; he was lost and is found.' So they began to celebrate.

[25]"Meanwhile, the older son was in the field. When he came near the house, he heard music and dancing. [26]So he called one of the servants and asked him what was going on. [27]'Your brother has come,' he replied, 'and your father has killed the fattened calf because he has him back safe and sound.'

[28]"The older brother became angry and refused to go in. So his father went out and pleaded with him. [29]But he answered his father, 'Look! All these years I've been slaving for you and never disobeyed your orders. Yet you never gave me even a young goat so I could celebrate with my friends. [30]But when this son of yours who has squandered your property

with prostitutes comes home, you kill the fattened calf for him!'

³¹"'My son,' the father said, 'you are always with me, and everything I have is yours. ³²But we had to celebrate and be glad, because this brother of yours was dead and is alive again; he was lost and is found.'"

4. What happened to the prodigal that brought him to his "senses" (v. 17)? How did this help his journey towards transformation?

5. Look at the prodigal's confession in verse 21. What does this confession say about the state of the prodigal's heart?

6. How did the prodigal become "alive," not "dead" (v. 31). What did being "alive" look like for the prodigal? What does being "alive" look like for you?

7. How does a person become more "alive" on the journey toward authentic transformation? What would they look like, feel like and act like?

8. Which of the two sons experienced authentic transformation? Explain your answer more fully.

EXPERIENCING THE JOURNEY

9. Look again at the table provided. What do you recognize about yourself as you read the section on pseudo-transformation?

10. What are you drawn to under authentic transformation?

EXPRESSING OUR HEARTS TO GOD

Read Psalm 51 as a prayer to God. Note particular phrases that David uses that express his longing for authentic transformation and restoration with God. Note especially verses 16-17 and David's own words to express what pleases God. Try to write Psalm 51:10-12 in your own words and expressing your own heart to God.

The only man I know who behaves sensibly is my tailor; he takes my measurements anew each time he sees me. The rest go on with their old measurements and expect me to fit them.

GEORGE BERNARD SHAW

THREE

TRANSFORMING THE PAST

There are two ways to kill a plant: You can cut it down, or you can just stop watering it.

As life requires input, manhood requires fathering. The father shapes a boy's sense of himself more deeply than any other person in his life. The father's absence, whether emotional or physical, has destructive effects.

Because all dads are imperfect, every man has a father-wound. For most of us, it's a nagging shame that we don't have the stuff of manhood: if other men find out we're weak, we'll be thrown off the team and cast into outer darkness. This brokenness between fathers and sons not only cripples individual men, it bears a curse on the larger society as well—in which men's God-given strength and creativity serve the Destroyer instead of the Creator. Transformation of a man's past must therefore begin with healing his father-wound.

EXPLORING MY STORY

1. How did your father or other male influencers shape your understanding of what it means to be a man?

2. How would you describe your "father-wound?"

3. How has your "father-wound" influenced your choices as a man? How has it affected your participation in the needs of your society?

ENGAGING THE SCRIPTURES
Matthew 3:13-17

[13]Then Jesus came from Galilee to the Jordan to be baptized by John. [14]But John tried to deter him, saying, "I need to be baptized by you, and do you come to me?"

[15]Jesus replied, "Let it be so now; it is proper for us to do this to fulfill all righteousness." Then John consented.

[16]As soon as Jesus was baptized, he went up out of the water. At that moment heaven was opened, and he saw the Spirit of God descending like a dove and lighting on him. [17]And a voice from heaven said, "This is my Son, whom I love; with him I am well pleased."

4. What did God say to Jesus and the crowd around him at his baptism?

I worship before You, dear Lord, as the all-wise Creator.... I praise You for the honor of being made in your image, personally formed by You for Your glory, and gifted spiritually just as it has pleased You. Thank You for each strength and ability and desirable trait You have give me. Surely You have been good to me, O Lord!

RUTH AND WARREN MEYERS

5. What would you imagine Jesus feeling upon hearing these statements?

6. How did this important message help set the stage for Jesus' life and ministry?

7. What difference does being called and knowing that you are the Beloved make in a person's life?

Self-rejection is the greatest enemy of the spiritual life because it contradicts the sacred voice that calls us the "Beloved."

HENRI NOUWEN

8. In what ways have you felt "beloved" by God? What difference does this make in your everyday life?

9. How can we live with this sense of true identity more in life?

EXPERIENCING THE JOURNEY

10. How can we affirm the true identity of our friends—who they are in God's eyes? What meaningful ways can you affirm your friends and family, reminding them of who they truly are in God's eyes?

11. Who do you trust to remind you who you are before God and others?

EXPRESSING OUR HEARTS TO GOD

God, how can I believe that I am so deeply loved by you when I have believed lies about myself and I feel so unworthy? Speak into my heart the truth of who I am and give me the assurance of your love. Help me to hear your voice calling *my* name and telling *me* of your great love. Give to me the courage to believe about myself what you have said is true of me. Help me to be a messenger of your love to those around me. Inspire me, O Lord, with creative ways of expressing their worth and belovedness. I pray in the name of the One whom you clearly called the Beloved: Jesus Christ, Amen.

TRANSFORMING OUR WOUNDS

The father-wound is a hook that Father God uses to draw us to himself. The man who can see clearly what his earthly dad did not give him will be more apt to ask God for it.

Yet often men deny their wound because we're taught to be strong, and a wound can make us feel weak and shameful. Too often, Christian men who recognize their childhood wound are afraid to talk about it, for fear of disobeying the commandment "Honor your father and your mother, so that you may live long in the land the LORD your God is giving you" (Exodus 20:12).

How do we move from being wounded to being transformed? This is a key and vital question in our journey. We can linger in aching pain for what *we did not* get or we can move through the pain to understanding and healing.

Forgiveness is the key to releasing the pain of your past and freeing yourself from its shame and fear. Denial short-circuits this process. A man who fancies, "My parents never hurt me" cannot forgive them, simply because he imagines he has nothing to forgive them for.

EXAMINING MY STORY

1. How has God used your past and pursued you through your wounds to bring you to himself?

2. In what ways is your wound still fresh? What do you still need from God as your wound heals?

ENGAGING THE SCRIPTURES:
Colossians 3:12-17

[12]Therefore, as God's chosen people, holy and dearly loved, clothe yourselves with compassion, kindness, humility, gentleness and patience. [13]Bear with each other and forgive whatever grievances you may have against one another. Forgive as the Lord forgave you. [14]And over all these virtues put on love, which binds them all together in perfect unity.

[15]Let the peace of Christ rule in your hearts, since as members of one body you were called to peace. And be thankful. [16]Let the word of Christ dwell in you richly as you teach and admonish one another with all wisdom, and as you sing psalms, hymns and spiritual songs with gratitude in your hearts to God. [17]And whatever you do, whether in word or deed, do it all in the name of the Lord Jesus, giving thanks to God the Father through him.

To forgive is to set a prisoner free and discover that the prisoner was you.

LEWIS B. SMEDES

3. Paul tells us to "clothe ourselves" (v. 12). List all the things Paul says we are to put on.

4. How does compassion relate to woundedness?

5. What does it mean when Paul says, "Forgive as the Lord forgave you"? When you think of God forgiving you, what image comes to mind?

6. What does forgiveness look like to you regarding your past? What expectations do you have about how a person should feel and act if they have dealt with their past?

> *He who cannot forgive breaks the bridge over which he himself must pass.*
>
> **GEORGE HERBERT**

7. How did Jesus practice forgiveness?

8. Paul says we are to "put on love." Putting on love doesn't mean that we should put on a façade. What does love look like?

9. How can Paul say, "Let the peace of Christ rule

in your hearts" when we consider the damage and wounding from our past? How does peace rule where pain exists?

10. There's a saying which says, "I can forgive, but I can't forget." Evaluate this statement in light of your understanding of practicing forgiveness in the way Jesus taught and modeled.

> Forgiveness is the answer to the child's dream of a miracle by which what is broken is made whole again, what is soiled is made clean again.
>
> DAG
> HAMMARSKJÖLD

EXPERIENCING THE JOURNEY

11. What would it look like to come to peace with your past? What would you need to do or stop doing?

12. Trace God's fingerprints through your past. How might God be using your past, no matter how painful it might have been, to bring you to himself?

Expressing Our Hearts to God

Read through this prayer before you say it, or something similar in your own words. Be as specific as you can about bringing to mind some thing, event or name that needs to be resolved.

Dear God,

Since you know all things, you know my past better than I do. You see my past, my past pain and my own failures to deal with my past well at all. You know the brokenness of my heart over issues that are not resolved and that cause me throbbing pain now in my heart. My pain grieves your heart as you understand sorrow and grief so well, through your own son, Jesus Christ.

I want to give you _____; it's too complicated and convoluted for me to understand. I place my past at your feet and ask that you transform it as you transform me, so that I can walk free. You are the God of transformation, and I give you thanks that you choose to continue this work in me now.

As long as we do not forgive those who wounded us, we carry them with us or, worse, pull them as a heavy load.

HENRI NOUWEN

FIVE

"HOW LONG IS ALL THIS CHANGE GOING TO TAKE?"

No two journeys are exactly alike. There's not a cookie-cutter way to transformation. No two journeys are exactly the same. Just as we are individually made, God uses many and varied ingredients in each person's journey towards transformation.

The image of a journey is seen throughout the Scriptures. Moses, Abraham, David, Jesus, Paul and more all journeyed through the wilderness, deserts, caves and more in search of God. The journey image especially helps us as we move through the changing seasons of life. When we experience doubt, apathy, disillusionment or depression, our first reaction is, "What did I do wrong?" The fact that my spiritual development is a journey explains these conditions as normal passages that we, as men, move through. Moses in the Midian wilderness; Joseph in the Egyptian prison; David hiding in caves; Daniel in the lions' den; Jonah in the belly of a fish; Job in the pit of despair; Jeremiah beaten and put in the stocks; Jesus on the cross.

Is it possible that what you are experiencing at this very moment is part of a journey that is being guided by your loving Father? Could it be that God is as interested in developing your faith as he was in developing Moses', Joseph's, and all the rest?

EXAMINING MY STORY

1. Choose a character in the Bible that you most identify with in terms of their journey and spiritual pilgrimage and explain why.

2. How does the image of a journey offer encouragement to you? What feelings surface when you think of where you've been so far on the journey?

3. How would you explain the place you are in right now in the journey? Choose an image, metaphor or geographical marking to describe your own journey.

ENGAGING THE SCRIPTURES

John 11:1-44

¹Now a man named Lazarus was sick. He was from Bethany, the village of Mary and her sister Martha. ²This Mary, whose brother Lazarus now lay sick, was the same one who poured perfume on the Lord and wiped his feet with her hair. ³So the sisters sent word to Jesus, "Lord, the one you love is sick."

[4]When he heard this, Jesus said, "This sickness will not end in death. No, it is for God's glory so that God's Son may be glorified through it." [5]Jesus loved Martha and her sister and Lazarus. [6]Yet when he heard that Lazarus was sick, he stayed where he was two more days.

[7]Then he said to his disciples, "Let us go back to Judea."

[8]"But Rabbi," they said, "a short while ago the Jews tried to stone you, and yet you are going back there?"

[9]Jesus answered, "Are there not twelve hours of daylight? A man who walks by day will not stumble, for he sees by this world's light. [10]It is when he walks by night that he stumbles, for he has no light."

[11]After he had said this, he went on to tell them, "Our friend Lazarus has fallen asleep; but I am going there to wake him up."

[12]His disciples replied, "Lord, if he sleeps, he will get better." [13]Jesus had been speaking of his death, but his disciples thought he meant natural sleep.

[14]So then he told them plainly, "Lazarus is dead, [15]and for your sake I am glad I was not there, so that you may believe. But let us go to him."

[16]Then Thomas (called Didymus) said to the rest of the disciples, "Let us also go, that we may die with him."

[17]On his arrival, Jesus found that Lazarus had already been in the tomb for four days. [18]Bethany was less than two miles from Jerusalem, [19]and many Jews had come to Martha and Mary to comfort them in the loss of their brother. [20]When Martha heard that

Jesus was coming, she went out to meet him, but Mary stayed at home.

[21]"Lord," Martha said to Jesus, "if you had been here, my brother would not have died. [22]But I know that even now God will give you whatever you ask."

[23]Jesus said to her, "Your brother will rise again."

[24]Martha answered, "I know he will rise again in the resurrection at the last day."

[25]Jesus said to her, "I am the resurrection and the life. He who believes in me will live, even though he dies; [26]and whoever lives and believes in me will never die. Do you believe this?"

[27]"Yes, Lord," she told him, "I believe that you are the Christ, the Son of God, who was to come into the world."

[28]And after she had said this, she went back and called her sister Mary aside. "The Teacher is here," she said, "and is asking for you." [29]When Mary heard this, she got up quickly and went to him. [30]Now Jesus had not yet entered the village, but was still at the place where Martha had met him. [31]When the Jews who had been with Mary in the house, comforting her, noticed how quickly she got up and went out, they followed her, supposing she was going to the tomb to mourn there.

[32]When Mary reached the place where Jesus was and saw him, she fell at his feet and said, "Lord, if you had been here, my brother would not have died."

[33]When Jesus saw her weeping, and the Jews who had come along with her also weeping, he was

deeply moved in spirit and troubled. [34]"Where have you laid him?" he asked.

"Come and see, Lord," they replied.

[35]Jesus wept.

[36]Then the Jews said, "See how he loved him!"

[37]But some of them said, "Could not he who opened the eyes of the blind man have kept this man from dying?"

[38]Jesus, once more deeply moved, came to the tomb. It was a cave with a stone laid across the entrance. [39]"Take away the stone," he said.

"But, Lord," said Martha, the sister of the dead man, "by this time there is a bad odor, for he has been there four days."

[40]Then Jesus said, "Did I not tell you that if you believed, you would see the glory of God?"

[41]So they took away the stone. Then Jesus looked up and said, "Father, I thank you that you have heard me. [42]I knew that you always hear me, but I said this for the benefit of the people standing here, that they may believe that you sent me."

[43]When he had said this, Jesus called in a loud voice, "Lazarus, come out!" [44]The dead man came out, his hands and feet wrapped with strips of linen, and a cloth around his face.

Jesus said to them, "Take off the grave clothes and let him go."

4. How would you describe the relationship between Jesus and Lazarus?

5. Describe Jesus' response when he heard that Lazarus was ill. How would you explain it?

6. Describe how Mary and Martha might have felt while they were waiting on Jesus to show up? What has it been like for you to want Jesus to do something for you or someone you love, yet he doesn't seem to show up on our time table?

7. Imagine Lazarus walking out from the tomb. From the text, what do you think he would have looked like?

8. How did Lazarus free himself of the strips of burial linen? Who helped to free him (v. 44)?

9. Describe how you would imagine Lazarus moved toward Jesus.

EXPERIENCING THE JOURNEY

10. How would you compare your present spiritual condition to Lazarus?

11. What is holding you back from moving to the One who promises you life over death?

12. Who can help free you of specific "graveclothes" that might be hindering your movement to Jesus?

EXPRESSING OUR HEARTS TO GOD

Sit quietly with this prayer. Pray about specific things and issues as they come to mind.

Dear Jesus:

I have tried to change so many times, yet I have failed. Call me forth from the tomb of pseudo-transformation. Hearing your voice gives me hope. Knowing that it is you who is calling me from death to life revives my heart. Strip the cloths away and set me free so that I can walk to you.

As I move to you, I understand that I will drag some old ways with me, but bring my friends around me so that I can truly be set free and be authentically transformed. I ask this in your name, not my own. Only in your name, Jesus Christ, is there power over my old ways and my old sin. I want to be set free.

THE JOURNEY AND THE DESTINATION

Tourists go wherever mood, pleasure or whim takes them. Pilgrims always have one eye on their destination, which gives meaning, hope and joy to their present place in the journey.

Having a clear picture of my destination allows me to make sense of my journey, even when I feel I am going in the opposite direction to what I had planned. Times of dryness or darkness are always difficult and challenging, but if I understand how they help me arrive at my ultimate destination I can welcome them as normal and necessary parts of my journey with Christ. Or, as Bernard of Clairvaux put it in the twelfth century, "When you have heard what the reward is, the labor of the climb will be less."

Seeing Jesus face to face and becoming like him—communion and union—are the two dimensions of our destination. As we walk with Christ, our communion with him deepens and matures. We become like Jesus by being with him. Living our life with him transforms us from the inside out.

EXAMINING MY STORY

1. How would you describe the destination of your journey?

2. What does a good journey look like? How does a person journey well through life?

3. What are the critical ingredients that a person needs to incorporate into their journey to finish well?

Spiritual growth does not happen at once. It is more like a developing fetus. Over time it becomes like a human shape, but even when it is born it is not perfect. Growth continues for years . . . spiritual progress is a continuing process. It is gradual, incremental.

PSEUDO-MACARIUS

ENGAGING THE SCRIPTURES
Jeremiah 18:1-6

[1]This is the word that came to Jeremiah from the LORD: [2]"Go down to the potter's house, and there I will give you my message." [3]So I went down to the potter's house, and I saw him working at the wheel. [4]But the pot he was shaping from the clay was marred in his hands; so the potter formed it into another pot, shaping it as seemed best to him.

[5]Then the word of the LORD came to me: [6]"O house of Israel, can I not do with you as this potter does?" declares the LORD. "Like clay in the hand of the potter, so are you in my hand, O house of Israel."

4. Imagine what Jeremiah witnessed.
    What did he see?

    What did he smell?

What did he hear?

What did he touch?

What did he taste?

5. What happened to the marred clay in the potter's hands? How can you see God using your marred clay in your life thus far?

6. What does the clay "do" in this process? What does the potter do?

EXPERIENCING THE JOURNEY

7. What is your role and responsibility in the process of spiritual transformation?

It is easy to imagine that we will get to a place where we are complete and ready, but preparation is not suddenly accomplished. It is a process steadily maintained. It is preparation and preparation.

OSWALD CHAMBERS

8. How might spiritual disciplines help in the process of transformation? Which ones have helped you thus far? How?

9. How can you be an encouragement to someone being reworked or re-formed in their own transformation?

10. What would "trusting the process" look like for you? How can you learn to trust the process of transformation more in your life?

> A journey involves process, action, movement, change, experiences, stops and starts, variety, humdrum, and surprises. For us a journey implies more than a quick trip from point A to point B. It is more extended, with the time and place between departure and final destination being important for their own sake.
>
> JANET O. HAGBERG AND ROBERT A. GUELICH

EXPRESSING OUR HEARTS TO GOD

Lord, it is good to remember that you are the Potter and I am the clay. I am reminded that my own transformation is not left up to me. Bring your hands and work in me the deep change you want. Shape me. Mold me. Transform me to what you would have me become.

I am available. I will sit here on this whirling wheel of life, work, past and desires, and ask you to transform my heart—all of it, including the marrings and repeated failures. Let your grace be poured out on me so that my heart can be softened and moldable.

You know, Lord, that my heart is sometimes hardened, sometimes brittle and sometimes fragile. Be tender when I need your care; be strong when I want to give up.

LEADER'S NOTES

Leading a group discussion can be an enjoyable and rewarding experience. But it can also be *scary*—especially if you've never done it before.

You don't need to be an expert on the Bible or a trained teacher to lead a Bible discussion. These studies are designed to be led easily. As a matter of fact, the flow of questions is so natural that you may feel that the studies lead themselves. Nevertheless, there are some important facts to know about group dynamics and encouraging discussion. The suggestions listed below should enable you to effectively and enjoyably fulfill your role as leader.

COMPONENTS OF SMALL GROUPS

A healthy small group should do more than study the Bible. There are four components to consider as you structure your time together.

Nurture. Small groups help us to grow in our knowledge and love of God. Bible study is important for making this happen.

Community. Small groups are a great place to develop deep friendships with other Christians. Allow time for informal interaction before and after each study. Plan activities and games that will help you get to know each other. Spend time having fun together.

Worship and prayer. Your study will be enhanced by spending time praising God together in prayer or song. Pray for each other's needs—and keep track of how God is answering prayer in your group. Ask God to help you to apply what you are learning together.

Outreach. Reaching out to others can be a practical way of applying what you are learning, and it will keep your group from becoming self-focused. Consider together what other men in your lives would benefit from your group experience, and encourage participants to invite and welcome newcomers at appropriate moments in the life of your group.

PREPARING FOR THE STUDY

1. Pray for the various members of the group—including yourself. Ask God to open your hearts to the message of his Word and motivate you to action.

2. As you prepare for each session, read and reread the assigned Bible passage to familiarize yourself with it. Look at the passage in multiple translations; you can do so quickly by using Bible Gateway online <www.biblegateway.com>.

3. Carefully work through each question in the session. Spend some time alone sitting quietly before God, asking him to lead you into creative ways of guiding the group and even your own heart.

4. Write your thoughts and responses in the space provided in the guide. This will help you to express yourself clearly.

5. It might help to have a Bible dictionary handy. Use it to look up any unfamiliar words, names or places.

6. Remember that the group will follow your lead in responding to these sessions. They will not go any deeper than you do.

7. Once you have finished your own study of the passage, familiarize yourself with the leader's notes for the study you are leading.

These are designed to help you in several ways. First, they tell you the purpose the author had in mind when writing the study. Take time to think through how the study questions work together to accomplish that purpose. Second, the notes provide you with additional background information or suggestions on group dynamics for various questions. This information can be useful when people have difficulty understanding or answering a question. Third, the leader's notes can alert you to potential problems you may encounter during the study.

8. If you wish to remind yourself of anything mentioned in the leader's notes, make a note to yourself below that question in the study.

LEADING THE STUDY

1. Begin the study on time. Open with prayer.

2. Be sure that everyone in your group has a study guide.

3. At the beginning of your first time together, explain that these sessions are meant to be discussions, not lectures. Encourage the members of the group to participate. However, do not put pressure on those who may be hesitant to speak during the first few sessions. You may want to suggest the following guidelines to your group:

    • Stick to the topic being discussed.

    • Anything said in the group is considered confidential and will not be discussed outside the group unless specific permission is given to do so.

    • Listen attentively to each other and provide time for each person present to talk.

    • Pray for each other.

4. Have a group member read the introduction at the beginning of the discussion.

5. Every session begins with questions to introduce the theme of the session and encourage group members to begin to open up. Either allow a time of silence for people to respond individually or discuss it together. Be ready to get the discussion going with your own response. You may want to supplement the group discussion question with an icebreaker to help people to get comfortable.

6. Have a group member (or members, if the passage is long) read aloud the passage to be studied. Then give people several minutes to read the passage again silently so that they can take it all in.

7. As you ask the questions, keep in mind that they are designed to be used just as they are written. You may simply read them aloud. Or you may prefer to express them in your own words. There may be times when it is appropriate to deviate from the study guide. For example, a question may have already been answered. If so, move on to the next question. Or someone may raise an important question not covered in the guide. Take time to discuss it, but try to keep the group from going off on tangents.

8. Avoid answering your own questions. If necessary, repeat or rephrase them until they are clearly understood. Or point out something you read in the leader's notes to clarify the context or meaning. An eager group quickly becomes passive and silent if they think the leader will do most of the talking.

9. Don't be afraid of silence. People may need time to think about the question before formulating their answers.

10. Don't be content with just one answer. Ask, "What do the rest of

you think?" or "Anything else?" until several people have given answers to the question.

11. Acknowledge all contributions. Try to be affirming whenever possible. Never reject an answer. If it is clearly off-base, ask, "What do the rest of you think?"

12. Don't expect every answer to be addressed to you, even though this will probably happen at first. As group members become more at ease, they will begin to truly interact with each other. This is one sign of healthy discussion.

13. Don't be afraid of controversy. It can be very stimulating. If you don't resolve an issue completely, don't be frustrated. Move on and keep it in mind for later. A subsequent study may solve the problem.

14. Periodically summarize what the group has said. This helps to draw together the various ideas mentioned and gives continuity to the group. But don't preach.

15. You may want to allow group members a time of quiet for "Experiencing the Journey" or "Expressing Our Hearts to God." Then discuss what you experienced. A simple way to do this is to ask the group to pray for a few moments in silence. Then, after an appropriate amount of time, just ask, "What did you tell God?" Or you may want to encourage group members to work on these ideas between meetings. Give an opportunity during the session for people to talk about what they are learning.

16. Conclude your time together with conversational prayer, adapting the prayer suggestion at the end of the study to your group. Ask for God's help in following through on the commitments you've made.

17. End on time.

THE VERY FIRST MEETING IS IMPORTANT!

Often, it's what happens in the initial meeting that determines the culture of the group. Here's a simple outline of the first group meeting.

1. Plan on addressing some or all of the ground rules. Decide how the group will function.

2. Make sure each group member has his own guide to use.

3. Read through the introduction to the guide as a group.

4. Ask an introductory question to help foster sharing:

   • What are your expectations about being in a group like this, studying a topic like this?

   • When you look at this topic, what gets stirred up inside of you?

   • What does your wife or girlfriend, if you have one, think about your studying this?

You're ready to begin the journey toward transformation!

SESSION ONE: *"Am I Ever Going to Change?"*

Question 1. You may find it helpful to ask group members to read through the sidebar quotes offered here, asking them if they identify with one in particular and why.

"Expressing Our Hearts to God." This prayer is taken from M. Robert Mulholland Jr., *Invitation to a Journey* (Downers Grove, Ill.: InterVarsity Press, 1993), p.19.

SESSION TWO: *Real Change*

Question 1. The table provided explores the difference between authentic transformation and pseudo-transformation. The biblical references are not exhaustive but will orient you to where and how the ingredients of transformation are discussed in Scripture. Refer to this table throughout the session, filling in further thoughts and impressions as the session continues.

Question 2. Give group members time to sit with this idea. The question isn't intended to point out failures in other people's attempts to change. Rather, it is meant to help you survey the lives of men you know to discern themes and patterns associated with authentic transformation: some simply may not work for you but did for another person. Have group members trace a specific issue that they have tried to change about themselves, "connecting the dots" about their desires, struggles, failures and successes in the journey. An example might be the struggle with sexual temptation, cursing or not being truthful. Encourage people to share with the group.

Question 4. Verse 17 implies a process in his transformation. See John 16:13 to explore the Spirit's role in our transformation.

Question 5. Compare the prodigal's statement, "I am not worthy to be called your son" to Ephesians 1:5, where Paul tells us God's plan for us to be adopted.

Question 6. See Ephesians 2:5 when Paul tells us we are made "alive" with Christ.

Question 7. If a person is to experience transformation, it's helpful to envision how a person's life would really change as God transforms him. Discuss how being transformed might affect a person's work, marriage, friendships, parenting.

"Expressing Our Hearts to God." David wrote this prayer of confession after he had committed adultery with Bathsheba and had her husband killed.

SESSION THREE: *Transforming the Past*

Question 2. If the term "father-wound" is new to group members, read Gordon Dalbey's chapter in *The Transformation of a Man's Heart* together. See Gordon Dalbey's *Healing the Masculine Soul* (Nashville: W Publishing, 2003) for a more thorough discussion on this subject.

Question 3. You may want to allow ten minutes in each session for one or two group members to share their story. This will keep the group moving and build personal stories into the life of your group.

Question 4. Have the group members read this passage from different translations, as the words may vary. God spoke publically so that Jesus could hear about being the "Beloved" and being the "delight" of God's heart.

Question 5. Jesus had led a relatively obscure life up until this particular time. Yet, upon his baptism and hearing this important message from God, everything changed for Jesus.

Question 7. Jesus was affirmed as the Beloved publicly and verbally. This message was repeated before a few of Jesus' disciples at the transfiguration (see Matthew 17:5). The Father-Son relationship described there and here between Jesus and God can become a model for our own healing from the wounds of the past.

Question 10. Allow some time for this. Be creative in affirming each person in the group. Allow each person to share what qualities they like and admire in each other, what they see in that person that reminds them of Jesus Christ, and so on.

SESSION FOUR: *Transforming Our Wounds*

Question 1. God uses the disappointment, pain and frustrations of our lives to create spiritual thirst and hunger in us. We can try many things in life to assuage the pain and hurt, yet we find that only Christ offers us what we really need. This question is meant to help men reflect on how God may have used or is still using something in our past to create within us a deeper desire to change our spiritual thirst.

Question 4. The word *compassion* comes from two words: "with" and "suffering." To have compassion is to attempt to enter into the suffering of another person. Hearing each other's stories of the father-wound will require compassion to listen and grace to respond.

Question 7. Jesus prayed, "Father, forgive them, for they do not know what they are doing" (Luke 23:34). This may be an appropriate prayer for men to pray on behalf of their own parents, or events that happened in our past.

Question 8. Read 1 Corinthians 13 as an example of what love looks like. Have group members think of someone who has wounded them and substitute their own name for the word *love*.

Question 9. See Philippians 4:7. Eugene Peterson puts it this way: "Before you know it, a sense of God's wholeness, everything coming together for good, will come and settle you down. It's wonderful what happens when Christ displaces worry at the center of your life."

Question 10. Be prepared for this to be a challenging time. Many men, when exploring their wounds initially, may find that anger, resentment, profound loss, disappointment and despair surface. These feelings need to be brought to Jesus. Throughout this study we want God's light to come and dispel our darkness.

Question 11. Offer some time for the group to sit in silence and reflect on these questions. After an appropriate length of time, ask the group to share what they have been thinking and processing.

Some group members need to start experiencing the many spiritual disciplines that Christians have practiced for years to experience transformation. For example, Henri Nouwen has said that "solitude is the furnace of transformation." For further discussion and study of this and other spiritual disciplines, refer to *Invitation to Solitude and Silence* by Ruth Haley Barton (Downers Grove, Ill.: InterVarsity Press, 2004); *Spiritual Disciplines Handbook: Practices That Transform Us* by Adele Calhoun (Downers Grove, Ill.: InterVarsity Press, 2005); Spiritual Disciplines Bible Studies by Jan Johnson (Downers Grove, Ill.: InterVarsity Press, 2003); and *Embracing Soul Care: Making Time for What Matters Most* by Stephen W. Smith (Grand Rapids: Kregel, 2006).

SESSION FIVE: *"How Long Is All This Change Going to Take?"*

Question 1. Some examples include Abraham's search for his new home; Moses' quest in bondage and trek in the wilderness; David's zigzagged journey of faith, passion, failure and forgiveness; Peter's upside down journey of zeal, dramatic encounters and denial of what was most sacred; Paul's zest for the mission's completion, enduring hardship for the sake of his call; or someone else.

"Engaging the Scriptures." This is a dramatic example of change! We can see that the movement of Lazarus toward Jesus holds hope for us in our own quest for transformation. His transformation wasn't clean and antiseptic. There was smell, lingering graveclothes and stumbling. He also had help from people under the direction of Jesus. Though this is a long passage, we will focus on one aspect of this dramatic incident. To help get the scene in perspective, have group members read four or five verses each aloud.

Question 4. See 11:3, 5, 11, 36. There was a significant relationship between Mary, Martha, Lazarus and Jesus. Evidently, Jesus was a frequent guest in their home when he came to town (see Matthew 26:6-12; Mark 14:3-9; Luke 10:38-42). This special friendship must have motivated Mary and Martha to find Jesus and to tell him that his friend Lazarus was very ill.

Question 6. Waiting on God can be a difficult experience, especially when God doesn't move on our demands or desires. Yet, something happens in our hearts when we wait that cannot happen at any other time. See Lamentations 3:25-30 for Jeremiah's words on how God uses waiting to transform us. Read from *The Message* if possible.

Question 7. Burial customs in Israel involved wrapping the body in strips of linen, pouring spices between the layers, before placing it in the tomb. The repeated reference to Lazarus' body being in the tomb for four days underscores the fact that Lazarus was dead, but also that bodily decay was already at work. When Lazarus walked out of the tomb, he did not emerge in ordinary street clothes. He came out with the strips of clothes still wound around his feet, body and hands.

Question 10. Answers may include "still in the tomb," "hearing Jesus calling but unable to move," "getting up as fast as I can," and "getting help to get free of the grave clothes."

Question 11. Read Hebrews 12:1-2 for another instance of being tangled up by something in our journey toward Jesus.

Question 12. Jesus specifically turned to those watching Lazarus emerge from the tomb to help him get free. Ask the group to explore how they can assist one another in their journey toward transformation.

SESSION SIX: *The Journey and the Destination*

Introduction. Taken from Bernard of Clairvaux, *Collected Works*, trans. G. R. Evans (New York: Paulist, 1987), p. 102.

"Engaging the Scriptures." The image of the potter and clay is one of the most frequently used metaphors in the Bible. This timeless image offers us an understanding of how God, as the Divine Potter, uses our mistakes to bring about transformation.

Question 5. Potters use the word *reclaiming* when they work with marred clay. They do not throw it away or discard it; rather, the marred clay is used again for the ultimate vision of what the potter has in mind.

Question 6. Other references about clay and the potter appear in Isaiah 64:8; 2 Corinthians 4:7-12.

Life is many things, but it is definitely not a flow chart. We prove it every day. We deeply long for change, but formulas and seminars don't get it done. The good news is, God is at work across the life span, encouraging us and empowering us to overcome the hurdles of our past, the challenges of our present and the fears of our future.

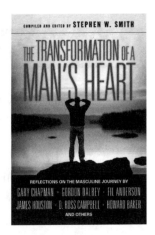

The Transformation of a Man's Heart is a book of stories: twelve men write from their hearts about their own journey toward transformation.

- Gary Chapman, author of **The Five Love Languages,** shares his journey toward experiencing a transformed marriage with his wife.

- Ross Campbell, Christian psychiatrist and author of **How to Really Love Your Child**, discusses his heart's transformation in growing as a father with his children.

- Gordon Dalbey pioneered the men's movement in his **Healing the Masculine Soul.** Here he shares how our past must be transformed in order to experience all God has for us as men.

- James Houston, mentor and friend to many Christian leaders throughout the world. considers how his own journey toward transformation reflects the call God places on every man's heart.

These and other leading men in their fields come alongside you in *The Transformation of a Man's Heart,* telling you their stories and pointing you toward the God who in the beginning wrote each of us a happy ending.

*"This book is full of stories. Some will make you think.
Others will make you cry. Still others will make you kneel.
All will make you want to be a better man."*

FROM THE FOREWORD BY KEN GIRE, AUTHOR OF *THE DIVINE EMBRACE*

TRANSFORMATION OF A MAN'S HEART SERIES

The Transformation of a Man's Heart series puts men in conversation with God and with one another to see how God shapes us in the ordinary experiences of our lives. The book, featuring reflections on the masculine journey by experts in a variety of fields, can be read independently or in concert with the four discussion guides, which look in depth at the role of sex, marriage, work and transformation in the spiritual lives of men.

Each guide has six sessions, suitable for personal reflection or group discussion and based on essays in the book *The Transformation of a Man's Heart.*

SEX

For all the attention we give it, sex remains a mystery. This discussion guide by Stephen W. Smith and John D. Pierce looks at sex as part of a man's transformational journey and explores how our sexual story can inform our understanding of God and his love for us.

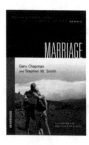

MARRIAGE

This discussion guide by Stephen W. Smith and Gary D. Chapman demystifies marriage for men, helping us see through the euphoria that led us to marry and the disillusionment that plagues us when our marriages don't turn out as we planned.

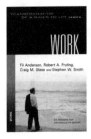

WORK

This discussion guide by Stephen W. Smith, Fil Anderson, Robert A. Fryling and Craig Glass puts men's vocational lives—their calling, their failings, their inheritance and their legacy—into the context of their relationship with God.

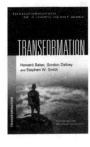

TRANSFORMATION

In this discussion guide by Stephen W. Smith, Gordon Dalbey and Howard Baker, men will be reminded that wherever they find themselves, God is there with them, inviting them out of their woundedness and onto a new and better path.

Potter's Inn is a Christian ministry founded by Stephen W. and Gwen Harding Smith, and is dedicated to the work of spiritual formation. A resource to the local church, organizations and individuals, Potter's Inn promotes the themes of spiritual transformation to Christians on the journey of spiritual formation by offering

- guided retreats
- soul care
- books, small group guides, works of art and other resources that explore spiritual transformation

Steve and Gwen travel throughout the United States and the world offering spiritual direction, soul care and ministry to people who long for a deeper intimacy with God. Steve is the author of *Embracing Soul Care: Making Space for What Matters Most* (Kregel, 2006) and *Soul Shaping: A Practical Guide to Spiritual Transformation*.

Potter's Inn at ASPEN RIDGE is a 35-acre ranch and retreat nestled in the Colorado Rockies near Colorado Springs, CO. As a small, intimate retreat, Potter's Inn at Aspen Ridge is available for individual and small group retreats. "Soul Care Intensives"—guided retreats with spiritual direction—are available for leaders in the ministry and the marketplace.

For more information or to for a closer look at our artwork and literature, visit our website: www.pottersinn.com

Or contact us at

Potter's Inn

6660 Delmonico Drive, Suite D-180

Colorado Springs, CO 80919

Telephone: 719-264-8837

Email: resources@pottersinn.com